Where It Leads

Also by Judith E.P. Johnson

Mountain Moods (VDL Publications, 1997)
Gatherers (VDL Publications, 1998)
Fragments (VDL Publications, 2000)
Selected Poems CD (7 RPH, 2001)
Snapshot (Regal Press, 2003)
Landmarks (Ginninderra Press, 2005)
Alone at the Window (Ginninderra Press, 2012)
Between Two Moons (Ginninderra Press, 2015)
Waking from Dreams (Ginninderra Press, 2016)

Judith E.P. Johnson

Where It Leads
haiku & senryu

Acknowledgements

Special thanks are due again to Peter Macrow for his kindness and inspiration; to my children Karen, Debra, and Craig for their support and encouragement; to Lyn Reeves for editing this book; and to Ron Moss for the art and design of the cover.

The author's haiku and senryu have been published in *Famous Reporter*, *Tasmanian Times*, *poam*, *paper wasp*, *Blue Giraffe*, *Shamrock*, *Windfall*, *Haiku Oz*, *Prospect*, *Still Heading Out*, *Poetry Matters*, *Poetic Reflections*, *Pause for Poetry* and *Kō*.

Where It Leads: haiku & senryu
ISBN 978 1 76041 540 2
Copyright © text Judith E.P. Johnson 2018

First published 2018 by
Ginninderra Press
PO Box 3461 Port Adelaide SA 5015
www.ginninderrapress.com.au

for Graeme

six a.m. news
I turn off murder and mayhem
birdsong

more talk of climate change
I watch the child
play with Noah's Ark

tickling my cheek
the child's butterfly kiss

stormy night
who is it
banging at my door?

cold gust
my neighbour invites children
to run through her leaves

across grassy paddocks
a ripple
of cloud shadows

blue sky, blue sea
all the yachts
leaning one way

alone
the wind
ruffles my hair

summer heat
dried snakeskin
on the barbed-wire fence

in and out
of leaf shadows
the fairy wren

high above
rocky cliffs
sea eagle drifting

childhood beach
how far away
the radiant mountain

rowing over clear waters
the sunlit flash
of fish

low tide
a soldier crab
disappears into the sand

just out of reach
gulls circle
a barking dog

Southern Lights
sky to sky
across the bay

on the shore
pelican
bigger than the toddler

deep-sea storm
Antarctic krill
washed up on the beach

on the divers' raft
a little pied cormorant
watches the water

stillness
behind dunes
the whining wind

sandstorm
I pick up the smoothness
of driftwood

dotterels
the beach awash
with cockle shells

twilight
the whisper of waves
and midden grasses

who made it?
this stone tool
in my hand

late frost
how tight the buds
in green leaves

sunburst
all those pink flowers
at my window

sudden breeze
hibiscus bush
a-twitter with finches

after rain
the smell of rain

across the lawn
leaves
from elsewhere

cottage garden
hollyhocks
taller than grandma

birdsong
from where
the scent of mock orange?

running round the pond
the child
follows a goldfish

gazing in the pond
my face
in the sky

through a crack
in the fence
the Wandering Jew

smell of mown grass
the hum
of a honeybee

blackberries
all the colours of autumn
on my tongue

day's end
leaves and sleeping birds
blend together

gift of silkworms
my neighbour and I
share a mulberry tree

how white
the cabbage moth
circling a red dahlia

cool breeze
curled under a leaf
the furry caterpillar

leafy hedge
a praying mantis stare
catches my eye

bird shadow
a slater
rolls into a ball

new resident
a green tree frog
in the flowerpot

native hen and chicks
somewhere
there's a nest

shining
in summer grasses
a Christmas beetle

capital city forecasts
only Hobart
has mountain snow

lunch in the park
suddenly
a gull on my knee

strangers in the street
stop to pat
each other's dogs

cold street
entering the salon
warmth of frangipani

Dark Mofo
in a ten-gallon drum
naked flame dancing

smoke haze
across the river
a ship's foghorn

hotel fireside
how icy
the gin and tonic

city lights
from somewhere
the scent of wattles

country road
we stop to watch
an echidna cross

shady bush track
trees link branches
overhead

tree-sky
the crunch of debris
under foot

far beneath a rock ledge
the sleeping snake

valley view
clouds
come and go

so close
the roar
of a distant waterfall

Organ Pipes
an eagle soars
into silence

wind
crying in the trees
where are you from?

feather light
in my palm
a wren's nest

walking through falling leaves
whispers of snow

pale sun
the wind rattles
the banksia trees

moon halo
rain clouds
cover the mountain

moonless night
a torch glows
in a one-man tent

warm breeze
children give the snowman
a new head

after the snowstorm
pink heath
half-buried

sunlight
through tree ferns
lace patterns on the snow

under ice
mountain stream
still flowing

bush midnight
only the stars

One Tree Point
even that tree
has gone

lounge room shelf
a line of ebony elephants
gathers dust

so cold the wax
on great grandmother's candlestick

roller-desk calendar
after New Year's Eve
says Turn Back

finishing
the book you gave me
I start again

standing silent
in a corner
grandfather clock

behind glass
butterflies from everywhere
pinned to a board

sunroom
the warm scent
of clothes airing

sunlit window square
on the floor
a glimpse of wings

old cookbook
I scratch-and-smell
sweet and sour pork

cards from grandchild
some of the glitter
on my face

in great-grandmother's workbox
her childhood thimble

cold night
mother puts a cosy
on the teapot

heavy cloud
only the rain
in my letter box

sky aglow
so silently
darkness falls

after the book reading
again
my room

winter night
you are my only companion
full moon

night winds
voices
from who knows where

clouds cover the moon
how can I read
your thoughts?

driving home
only our headlights
and the moon

so we meet again
blue moon

moving
through morning darkness
colours of light

wherever I go
following me
my ancestors

nativity service
my sister's baby
in the crib

moonlight
in the doll's house
tiny shadows

where it leads
this winding path

www.ingramcontent.com/pod-product-compliance
Lightning Source LLC
Chambersburg PA
CBHW070051120526
44589CB00034B/1992